2026

January
S	M	T	W	T	F	S
				1	2	3
4	5	6	7	8	9	10
11	12	13	14	15	16	17
18	19	20	21	22	23	24
25	26	27	28	29	30	31

February
S	M	T	W	T	F	S
1	2	3	4	5	6	7
8	9	10	11	12	13	14
15	16	17	18	19	20	21
22	23	24	25	26	27	28

March
S	M	T	W	T	F	S
1	2	3	4	5	6	7
8	9	10	11	12	13	14
15	16	17	18	19	20	21
22	23	24	25	26	27	28
29	30	31				

April
S	M	T	W	T	F	S
			1	2	3	4
5	6	7	8	9	10	11
12	13	14	15	16	17	18
19	20	21	22	23	24	25
26	27	28	29	30		

May
S	M	T	W	T	F	S
					1	2
3	4	5	6	7	8	9
10	11	12	13	14	15	16
17	18	19	20	21	22	23
24	25	26	27	28	29	30
31						

June
S	M	T	W	T	F	S
	1	2	3	4	5	6
7	8	9	10	11	12	13
14	15	16	17	18	19	20
21	22	23	24	25	26	27
28	29	30				

July
S	M	T	W	T	F	S
			1	2	3	4
5	6	7	8	9	10	11
12	13	14	15	16	17	18
19	20	21	22	23	24	25
26	27	28	29	30	31	

August
S	M	T	W	T	F	S
						1
2	3	4	5	6	7	8
9	10	11	12	13	14	15
16	17	18	19	20	21	22
23	24	25	26	27	28	29
30	31					

September
S	M	T	W	T	F	S
		1	2	3	4	5
6	7	8	9	10	11	12
13	14	15	16	17	18	19
20	21	22	23	24	25	26
27	28	29	30			

October
S	M	T	W	T	F	S
				1	2	3
4	5	6	7	8	9	10
11	12	13	14	15	16	17
18	19	20	21	22	23	24
25	26	27	28	29	30	31

November
S	M	T	W	T	F	S
1	2	3	4	5	6	7
8	9	10	11	12	13	14
15	16	17	18	19	20	21
22	23	24	25	26	27	28
29	30					

December
S	M	T	W	T	F	S
		1	2	3	4	5
6	7	8	9	10	11	12
13	14	15	16	17	18	19
20	21	22	23	24	25	26
27	28	29	30	31		

JANUARY

SUNDAY	MONDAY	TUESDAY	WEDNESDAY
4	5	6	7
11	12	13	14
18	19 Martin Luther King Day(US)	20	21
25	26	27	28

2026

THURSDAY	FRIDAY	SATURDAY	NOTES
1 New Years's Day	2	3	
8	9	10	
15	16	17	
22	23	24	
29	30	31	

weekly journal

MONDAY

TUESDAY

WEDNESDAY

WEEK OF: _____

THURSDAY

FRIDAY

SATURDAY

SUNDAY

weekly journal

MONDAY

TUESDAY

WEDNESDAY

WEEK OF: _____

THURSDAY

FRIDAY

SATURDAY

SUNDAY

weekly journal

MONDAY

TUESDAY

WEDNESDAY

WEEK OF: _____

THURSDAY

FRIDAY

SATURDAY

SUNDAY

weekly journal

MONDAY

TUESDAY

WEDNESDAY

WEEK OF: _____

THURSDAY

FRIDAY

SATURDAY

SUNDAY

weekly journal

MONDAY

TUESDAY

WEDNESDAY

WEEK OF: _____

THURSDAY

FRIDAY

SATURDAY

SUNDAY

FEBRUARY

SUNDAY	MONDAY	TUESDAY	WEDNESDAY
1	2	3	4
8	9	10	11
15	16 Presidents' Day(US)	17 Ramadan Chinese NewYear	18
22	23	24	25

2026

THURSDAY	FRIDAY	SATURDAY	NOTES
5	6	7	
12	13	14	
19	20	21 Valentine's Day	
26	27	28	

weekly journal

MONDAY

TUESDAY

WEDNESDAY

WEEK OF: _____

THURSDAY

FRIDAY

SATURDAY

SUNDAY

weekly journal

MONDAY

TUESDAY

WEDNESDAY

WEEK OF: _____

THURSDAY

FRIDAY

SATURDAY

SUNDAY

weekly journal

MONDAY

TUESDAY

WEDNESDAY

WEEK OF: _____

THURSDAY

FRIDAY

SATURDAY

SUNDAY

weekly journal

MONDAY

TUESDAY

WEDNESDAY

WEEK OF: _____

THURSDAY

FRIDAY

SATURDAY

SUNDAY

weekly journal

MONDAY

TUESDAY

WEDNESDAY

WEEK OF: _____

THURSDAY

FRIDAY

SATURDAY

SUNDAY

MARCH

SUNDAY	MONDAY	TUESDAY	WEDNESDAY
1	2	3	4
8	9	10	11
15	16	17 Saint Patrick's Day	18
22	23	24	25
29	30	31	

2026

THURSDAY	FRIDAY	SATURDAY	NOTES
5	6	7	
12	13	14	
19	20	21	
26	27	28	

weekly journal

MONDAY

TUESDAY

WEDNESDAY

WEEK OF: _____

THURSDAY

FRIDAY

SATURDAY

SUNDAY

weekly journal

MONDAY

TUESDAY

WEDNESDAY

WEEK OF: _____

THURSDAY

FRIDAY

SATURDAY

SUNDAY

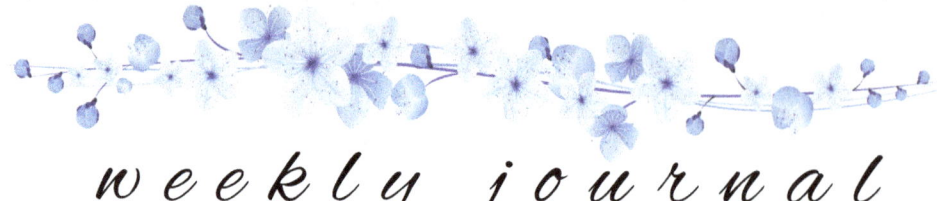

weekly journal

MONDAY

TUESDAY

WEDNESDAY

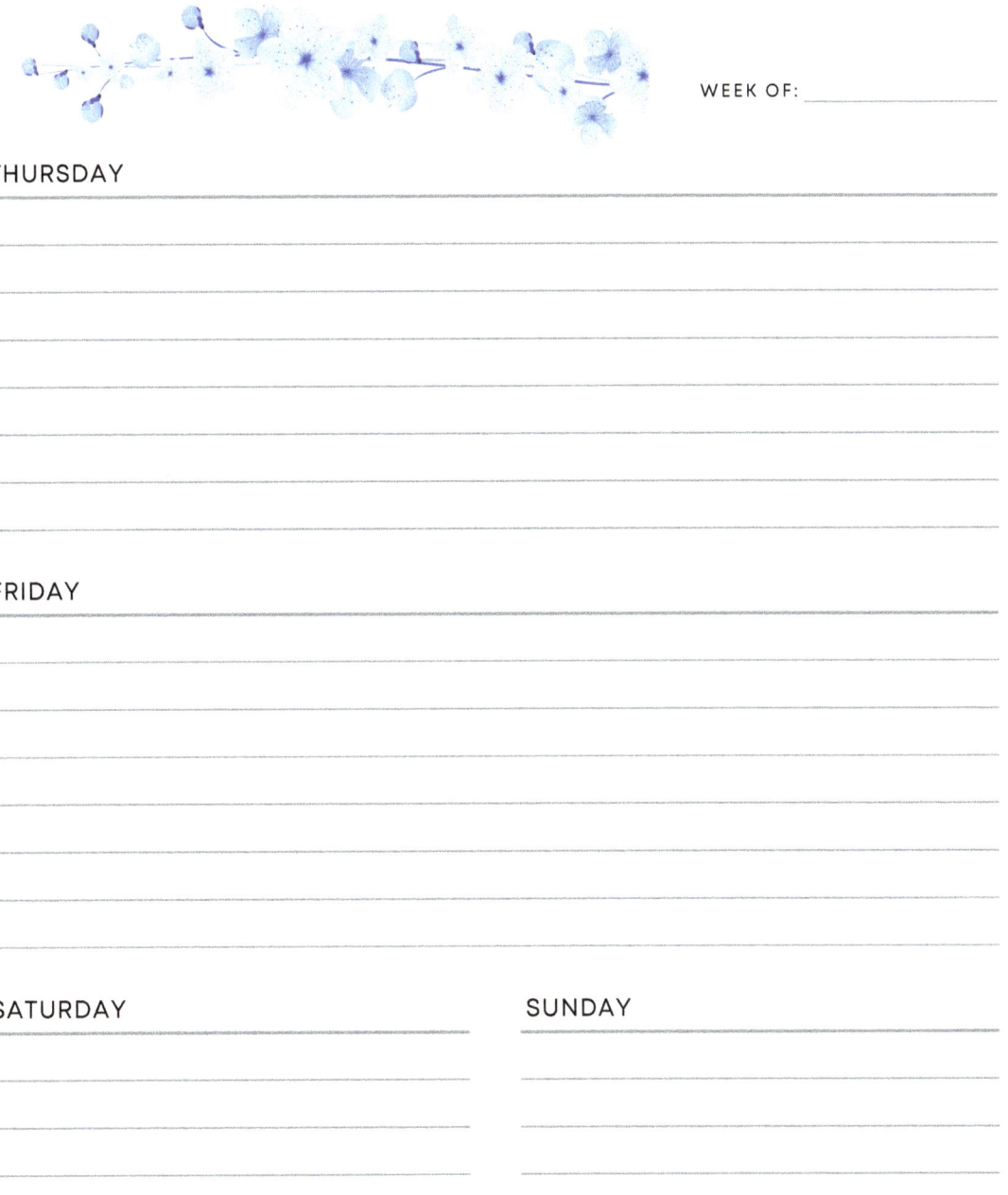

WEEK OF: _____

THURSDAY

FRIDAY

SATURDAY

SUNDAY

weekly journal

MONDAY

TUESDAY

WEDNESDAY

WEEK OF: _____

THURSDAY

FRIDAY

SATURDAY

SUNDAY

weekly journal

MONDAY

TUESDAY

WEDNESDAY

WEEK OF: _____

THURSDAY

FRIDAY

SATURDAY

SUNDAY

APRIL

SUNDAY	MONDAY	TUESDAY	WEDNESDAY
			1
			Passover Eve
5	6	7	8
Easter Sunday	Easter Monday		
12	13	14	15
19	20	21	22
26	27	28	29

2026

THURSDAY	FRIDAY	SATURDAY	NOTES
2	3 Good Friday	4	
9	10	11	
Last Day of Passover			
16	17	18	
23	24	25	
30			

weekly journal

MONDAY

TUESDAY

WEDNESDAY

WEEK OF: _____

THURSDAY

FRIDAY

SATURDAY

SUNDAY

weekly journal

MONDAY

TUESDAY

WEDNESDAY

WEEK OF: _____

THURSDAY

FRIDAY

SATURDAY

SUNDAY

weekly journal

MONDAY

TUESDAY

WEDNESDAY

WEEK OF: _____

THURSDAY

FRIDAY

SATURDAY

SUNDAY

weekly journal

MONDAY

TUESDAY

WEDNESDAY

WEEK OF: _____

THURSDAY

FRIDAY

SATURDAY

SUNDAY

weekly journal

MONDAY

TUESDAY

WEDNESDAY

WEEK OF: _____

THURSDAY

FRIDAY

SATURDAY

SUNDAY

MAY

SUNDAY	MONDAY	TUESDAY	WEDNESDAY
3	4	5 Cinco de Mayo(US)	6
10 Mother's Day	11	12	13
17	18	19	20
24	25 Memorial Day(US)	26	27
31			

2026

THURSDAY	FRIDAY	SATURDAY	NOTES
	1	2	
7	8	9	
14	15	16	
21	22	23	
28	29	30	

weekly journal

MONDAY

TUESDAY

WEDNESDAY

WEEK OF: _____

THURSDAY

FRIDAY

SATURDAY

SUNDAY

weekly journal

MONDAY

TUESDAY

WEDNESDAY

WEEK OF: _____

THURSDAY

FRIDAY

SATURDAY

SUNDAY

weekly journal

MONDAY

TUESDAY

WEDNESDAY

WEEK OF: _____

THURSDAY

FRIDAY

SATURDAY

SUNDAY

weekly journal

MONDAY

TUESDAY

WEDNESDAY

WEEK OF: _____

THURSDAY

FRIDAY

SATURDAY

SUNDAY

weekly journal

MONDAY

TUESDAY

WEDNESDAY

WEEK OF: _____

THURSDAY

FRIDAY

SATURDAY

SUNDAY

JUNE

SUNDAY	MONDAY	TUESDAY	WEDNESDAY
	1	2	3
7	8	9	10
14	15	16	17
21 Father's Day	22	23	24
28	29	30	

2026

THURSDAY	FRIDAY	SATURDAY	NOTES
4	5	6	
11	12	13	
18	19 Juneteenth (US)	20	
25	26	27	

weekly journal

MONDAY

TUESDAY

WEDNESDAY

WEEK OF: _____

THURSDAY

FRIDAY

SATURDAY

SUNDAY

weekly journal

MONDAY

TUESDAY

WEDNESDAY

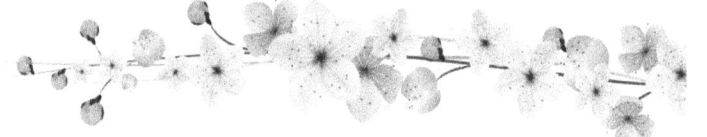

WEEK OF: _____

THURSDAY

FRIDAY

SATURDAY

SUNDAY

weekly journal

MONDAY

TUESDAY

WEDNESDAY

WEEK OF: _____

THURSDAY

FRIDAY

SATURDAY

SUNDAY

weekly journal

MONDAY

TUESDAY

WEDNESDAY

WEEK OF: _____

THURSDAY

FRIDAY

SATURDAY

SUNDAY

weekly journal

MONDAY

TUESDAY

WEDNESDAY

WEEK OF: _____

THURSDAY

FRIDAY

SATURDAY

SUNDAY

JULY

SUNDAY	MONDAY	TUESDAY	WEDNESDAY
			1
5	6	7	8
12	13	14	15
19	20	21	22
26	27	28	29

2026

THURSDAY	FRIDAY	SATURDAY	NOTES
2	3	4 Independence Day(US)	
9	10	11	
16	17	18	
23	24	25	
30	31		

weekly journal

MONDAY

TUESDAY

WEDNESDAY

WEEK OF: _____

THURSDAY

FRIDAY

SATURDAY

SUNDAY

weekly journal

MONDAY

TUESDAY

WEDNESDAY

WEEK OF: _____

THURSDAY

FRIDAY

SATURDAY

SUNDAY

weekly journal

MONDAY

TUESDAY

WEDNESDAY

WEEK OF: _____

THURSDAY

FRIDAY

SATURDAY

SUNDAY

weekly journal

MONDAY

TUESDAY

WEDNESDAY

WEEK OF: _____

THURSDAY

FRIDAY

SATURDAY

SUNDAY

weekly journal

MONDAY

TUESDAY

WEDNESDAY

WEEK OF: _____

THURSDAY

FRIDAY

SATURDAY

SUNDAY

AUGUST

SUNDAY	MONDAY	TUESDAY	WEDNESDAY
2	3	4	5
9	10	11	12
16	17	18	19
23	24	25	26
30	31		

2026

THURSDAY	FRIDAY	SATURDAY	NOTES
		1	
6	7	8	
13	14	15	
20	21	22	
27	28	29	

weekly journal

MONDAY

TUESDAY

WEDNESDAY

WEEK OF: _____

THURSDAY

FRIDAY

SATURDAY

SUNDAY

weekly journal

MONDAY

TUESDAY

WEDNESDAY

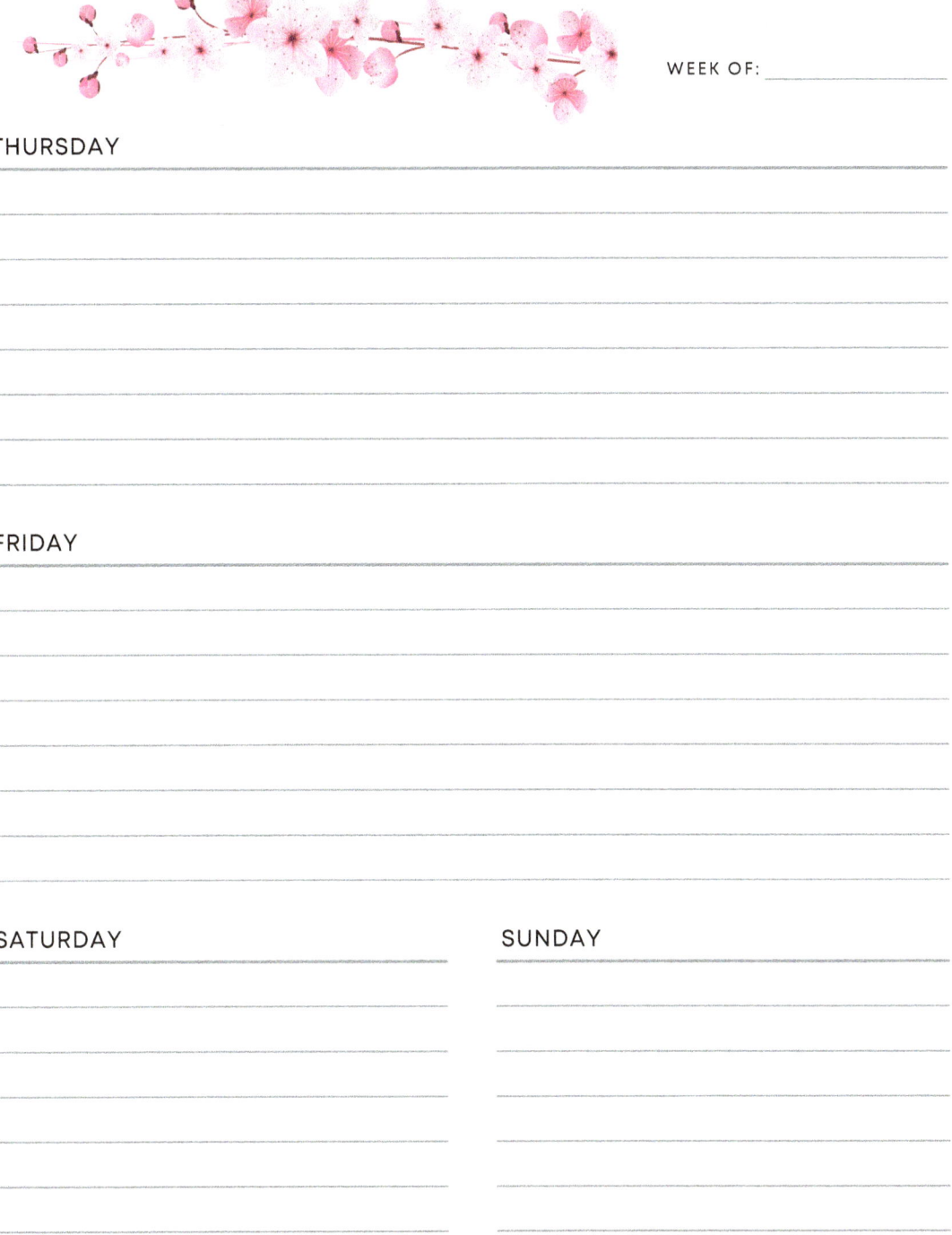

WEEK OF: _____

THURSDAY

FRIDAY

SATURDAY

SUNDAY

weekly journal

MONDAY

TUESDAY

WEDNESDAY

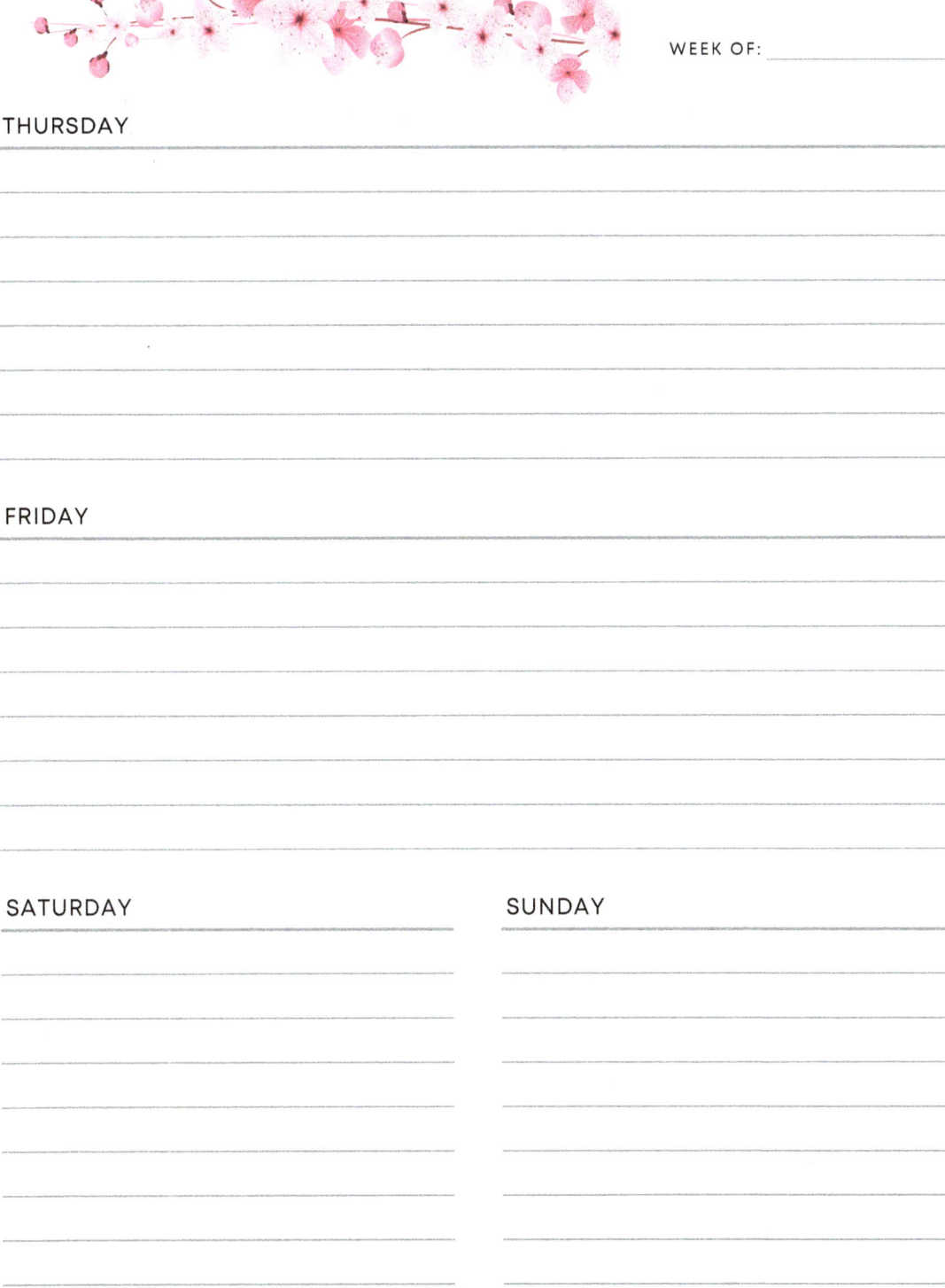

WEEK OF: _____

THURSDAY

FRIDAY

SATURDAY

SUNDAY

weekly journal

MONDAY

TUESDAY

WEDNESDAY

WEEK OF: _____

THURSDAY

FRIDAY

SATURDAY

SUNDAY

weekly journal

MONDAY

TUESDAY

WEDNESDAY

WEEK OF: _____

THURSDAY

FRIDAY

SATURDAY

SUNDAY

SEPTEMBER

SUNDAY	MONDAY	TUESDAY	WEDNESDAY
		1	2
6	7 Labor Day(US)	8	9
13	14	15	16
20	21	22	23
27	28 Yom Kippur	29	30

2026

THURSDAY	FRIDAY	SATURDAY	NOTES
3	4	5	
10	11	12	
17	18	19 Rosh Hashana	
24	25	26	

weekly journal

MONDAY

TUESDAY

WEDNESDAY

WEEK OF: _____

THURSDAY

FRIDAY

SATURDAY

SUNDAY

weekly journal

MONDAY

TUESDAY

WEDNESDAY

WEEK OF: _____

THURSDAY

FRIDAY

SATURDAY

SUNDAY

weekly journal

MONDAY

TUESDAY

WEDNESDAY

WEEK OF: _____

THURSDAY

FRIDAY

SATURDAY

SUNDAY

weekly journal

MONDAY

TUESDAY

WEDNESDAY

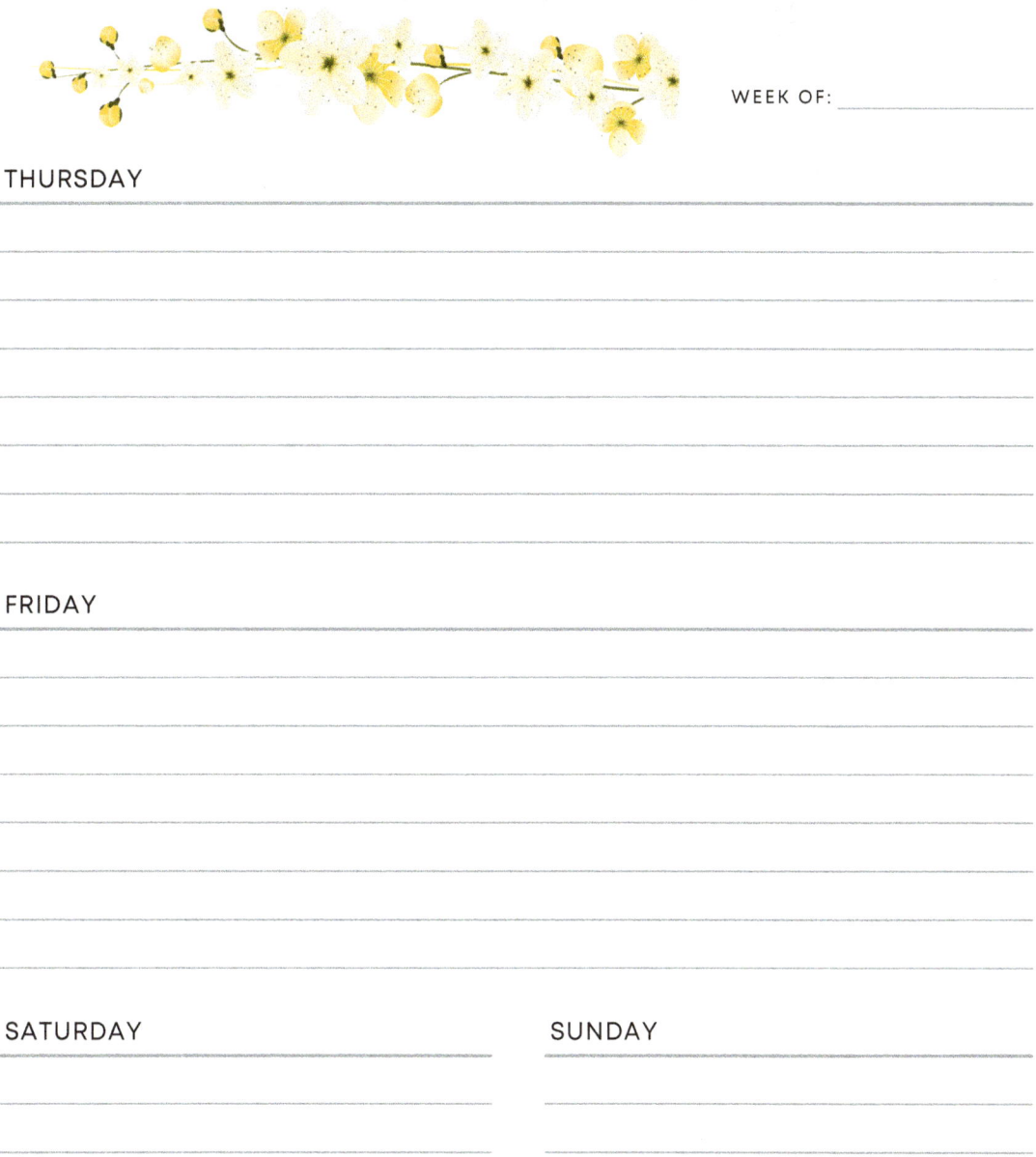

WEEK OF: _____

THURSDAY

FRIDAY

SATURDAY

SUNDAY

weekly journal

MONDAY

TUESDAY

WEDNESDAY

WEEK OF: _____

THURSDAY

FRIDAY

SATURDAY

SUNDAY

OCTOBER

SUNDAY	MONDAY	TUESDAY	WEDNESDAY
4	5	6	7
11	12	13	14
18	19	20	21
25	26	27	28

2026

THURSDAY	FRIDAY	SATURDAY	NOTES
1	2	3	
8	9	10	
15	16	17	
22	23	24	
29	30	31 Halloween	

weekly journal

MONDAY

TUESDAY

WEDNESDAY

WEEK OF: _____

THURSDAY

FRIDAY

SATURDAY

SUNDAY

weekly journal

MONDAY

TUESDAY

WEDNESDAY

WEEK OF: _____

THURSDAY

FRIDAY

SATURDAY

SUNDAY

weekly journal

MONDAY

TUESDAY

WEDNESDAY

WEEK OF: _____

THURSDAY

FRIDAY

SATURDAY

SUNDAY

weekly journal

MONDAY

TUESDAY

WEDNESDAY

WEEK OF: _____

THURSDAY

FRIDAY

SATURDAY

SUNDAY

weekly journal

MONDAY

TUESDAY

WEDNESDAY

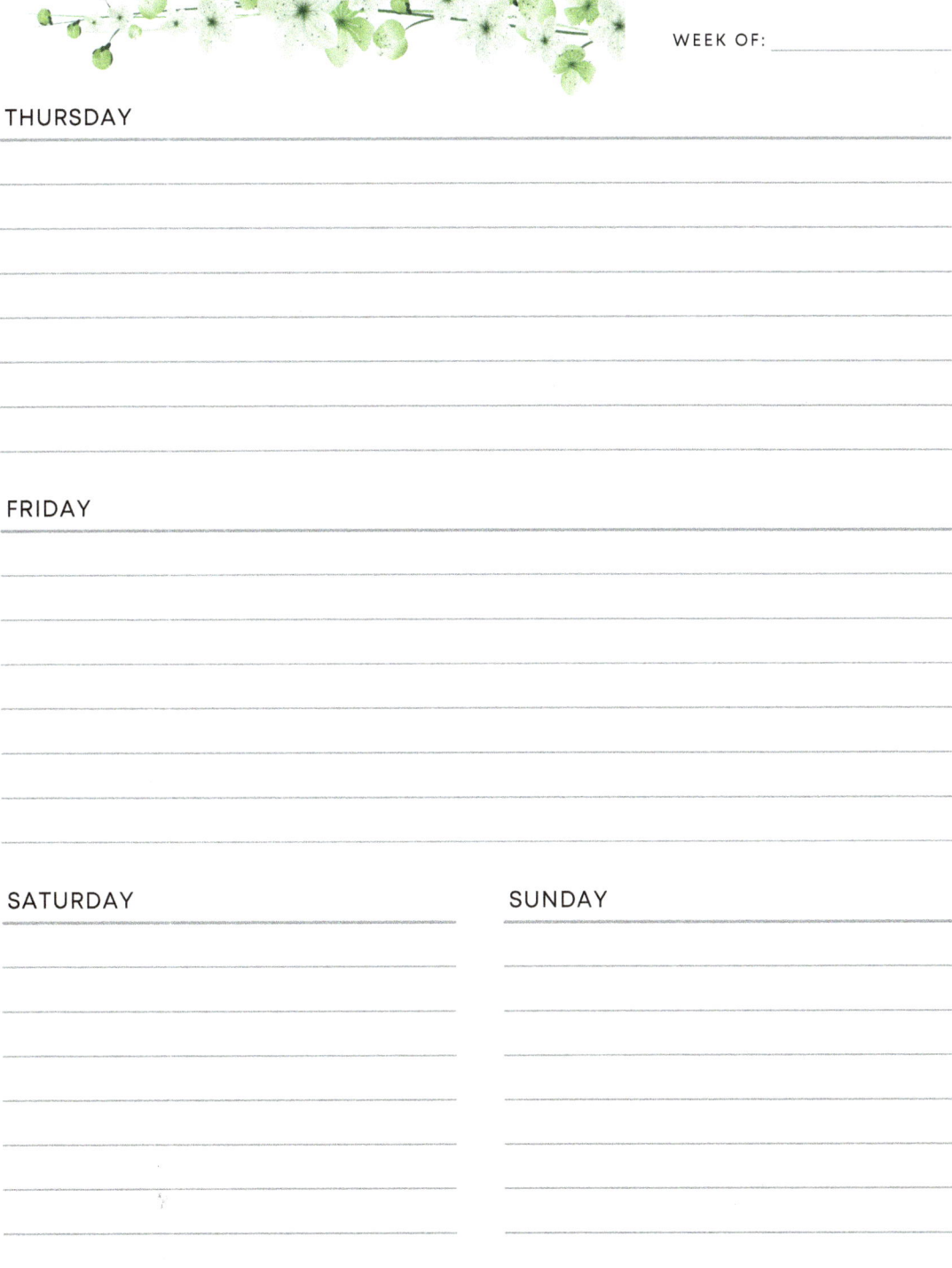

WEEK OF: _____

THURSDAY

FRIDAY

SATURDAY

SUNDAY

NOVEMBER

SUNDAY	MONDAY	TUESDAY	WEDNESDAY
1	2	3	4
8	9	10	11 *Veterans Day(US)*
15	16	17	18
22	23	24	25
29	30 *Cyber Monday*		

2026

THURSDAY	FRIDAY	SATURDAY	NOTES
5	6	7	
12	13	14	
19	20	21	
26 Thanksgiving Day (US)	27 Black Friday	28	

weekly journal

MONDAY

TUESDAY

WEDNESDAY

WEEK OF: _____

THURSDAY

FRIDAY

SATURDAY

SUNDAY

weekly journal

MONDAY

TUESDAY

WEDNESDAY

WEEK OF: _____

THURSDAY

FRIDAY

SATURDAY

SUNDAY

weekly journal

MONDAY

TUESDAY

WEDNESDAY

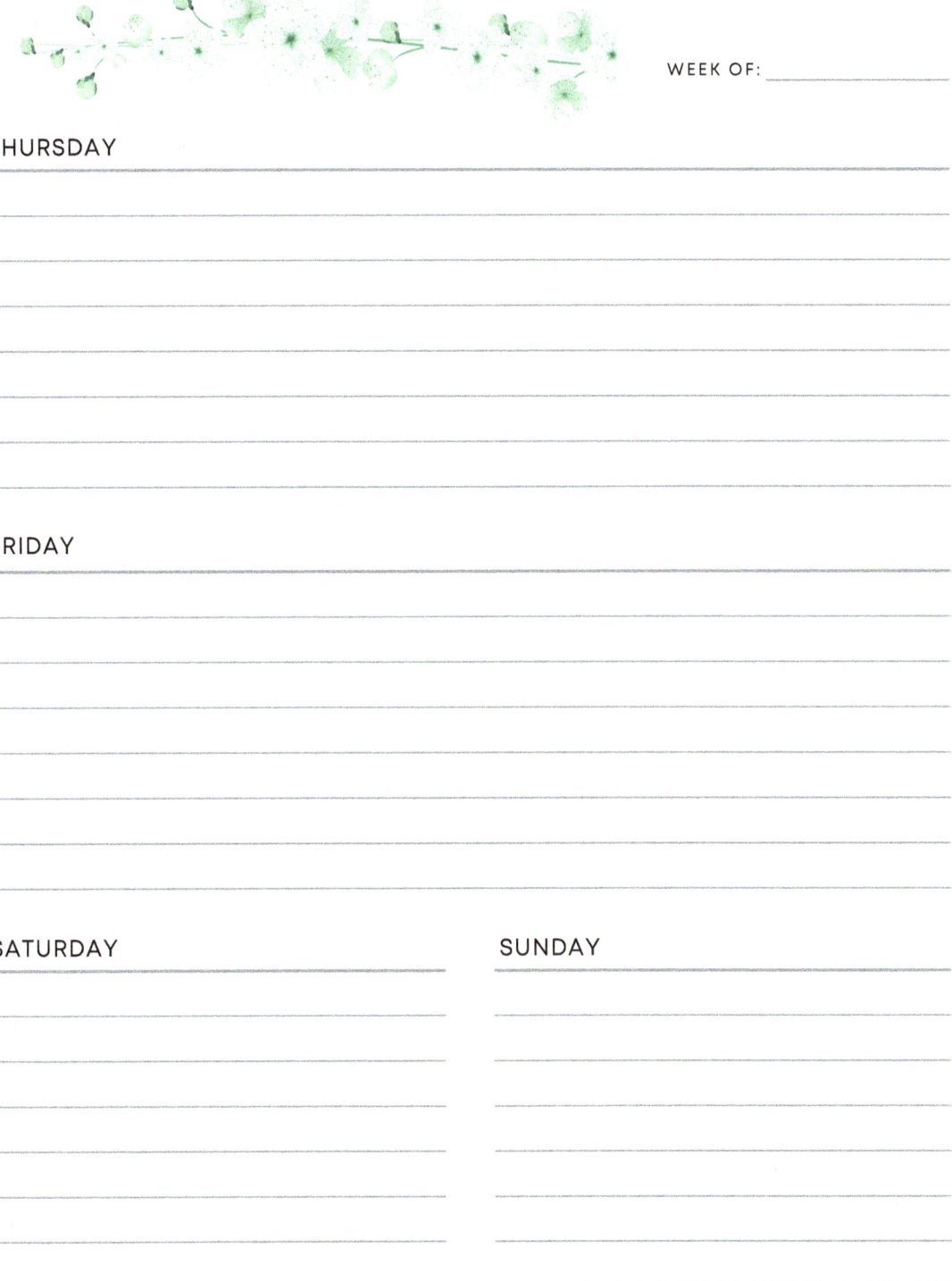

WEEK OF: _____

THURSDAY

FRIDAY

SATURDAY

SUNDAY

weekly journal

MONDAY

TUESDAY

WEDNESDAY

WEEK OF: _____

THURSDAY

FRIDAY

SATURDAY

SUNDAY

weekly journal

MONDAY

TUESDAY

WEDNESDAY

WEEK OF: _____

THURSDAY

FRIDAY

SATURDAY

SUNDAY

DECEMBER

SUNDAY	MONDAY	TUESDAY	WEDNESDAY
		1	2
6	7	8	9
13	14	15	16
20	21	22	23
27	28	29	30

2026

THURSDAY	FRIDAY	SATURDAY	NOTES
3	4	5 *First Day of Hannukah*	
10	11	12 *Last Day of Hannukah*	
17	18	19	
24 *Christmas Eve*	25 *Christmas Day*	26	
31 *New Year's Eve*			

weekly journal

MONDAY

TUESDAY

WEDNESDAY

WEEK OF: _____

THURSDAY

FRIDAY

SATURDAY

SUNDAY

weekly journal

MONDAY

TUESDAY

WEDNESDAY

WEEK OF: _____

THURSDAY

FRIDAY

SATURDAY

SUNDAY

weekly journal

MONDAY

TUESDAY

WEDNESDAY

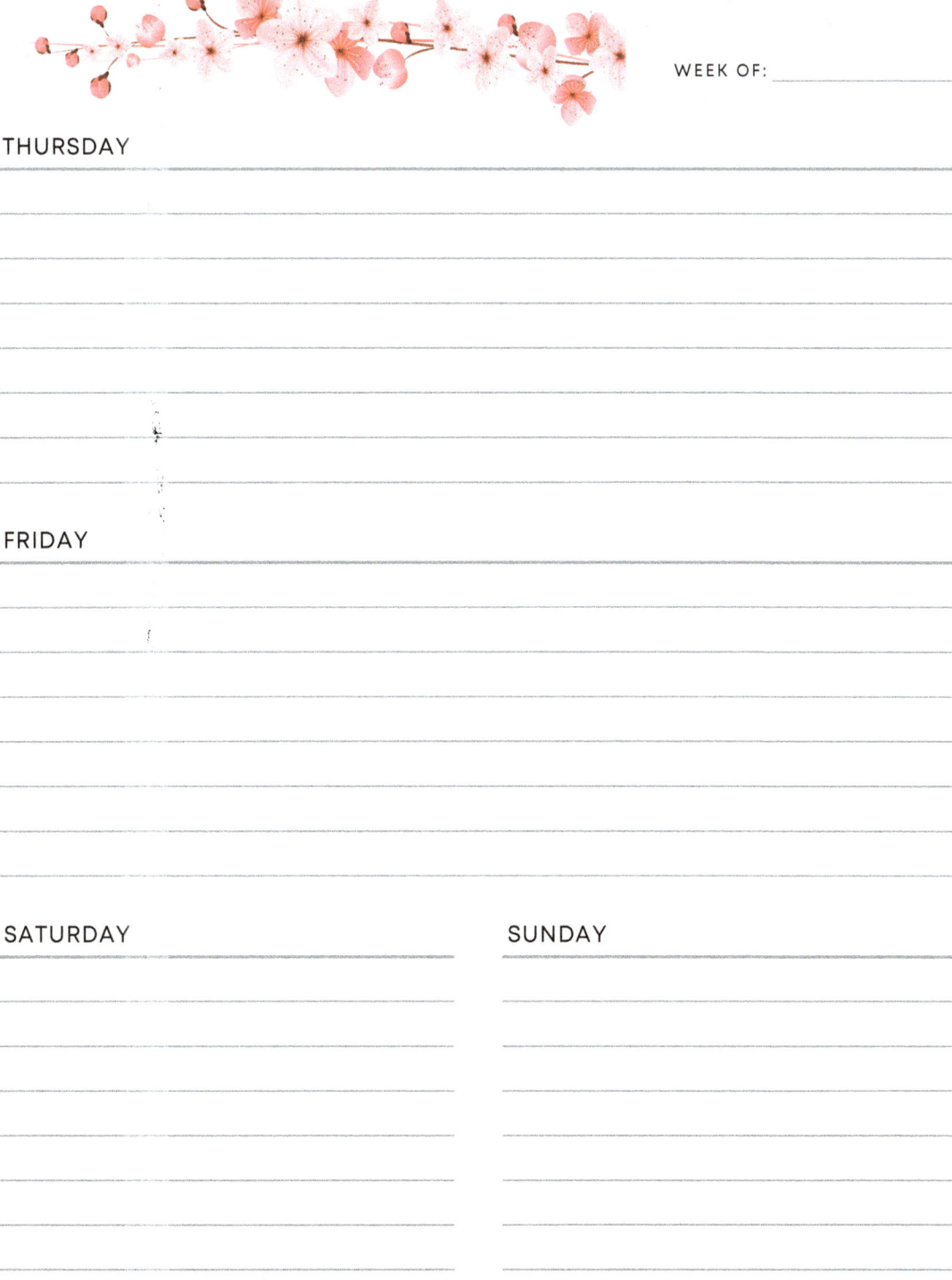

WEEK OF: _____

THURSDAY

FRIDAY

SATURDAY

SUNDAY

weekly journal

MONDAY

TUESDAY

WEDNESDAY

WEEK OF: _____

THURSDAY

FRIDAY

SATURDAY

SUNDAY

weekly journal

MONDAY

TUESDAY

WEDNESDAY

WEEK OF: _____

THURSDAY

FRIDAY

SATURDAY

SUNDAY

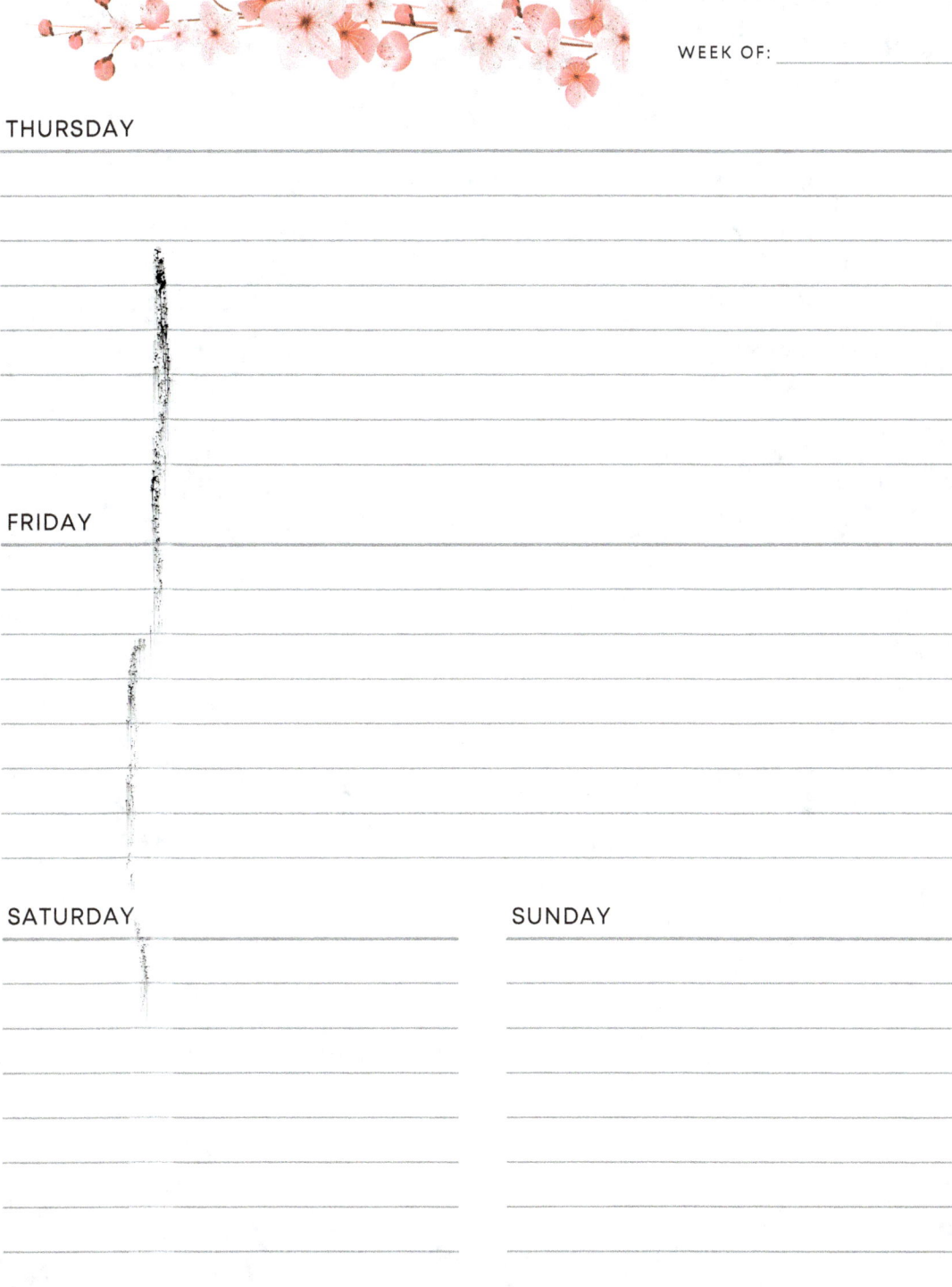

www.ingramcontent.com/pod-product-compliance
Lightning Source LLC
Chambersburg PA
CBHW081429070526
44586CB00020B/2528